I started writing poetry as my 60th birthd[...] of those rather special and unexpected tim[...] happens out of the blue. It came in the s[...] workshop at a course I was attending. As [...] first poem 'It's Good Innit?' Previous to that I had never considered writing poetry. Since then I haven't stopped.

As I ventured enthusiastically into this new world I found people to be my main inspiration. Some of these individuals I've met through my work as a counsellor, some through other work and some are family members. Other poems are based on observation or opinion.

I sincerely hope you enjoy this book.

June 2016.

To

Linda

Best wishes

Catherine Scott

A Woman With A View

Catherine Scott

Illustrated by Matt Mullen

Burning Eye

This edition published by Burning Eye Books 2013

www.burningeye.co.uk

@burningeye

Burning Eye Books
15 West Hill, Portishead, BS20 6LG

ISBN 978 1 90913 623 6

Printed in Scotland by Bell & Bain, Glasgow

CONTENTS

HULL
It's Good Innit?   9
Who Do They Think They Are?   10

RELATIONSHIPS
A Nice Young Man   12
Unrequited Love   14
Do You?   16
The Honeymoon Period   17
Is It Me?   18
He's Going To Get It   20
I'm Leaving You   22
Me Dad   24
Ode To The Flat Cap   26
My Daughter Is Getting Married   28
Sweary Mary   29

NOSTALGIA AND FOOD
Those Were The Days   32
There Were No Computers   34
My Mum's Cooking   36
Let Us Eat Cake   37
Doncaster Butterscotch   38
Buzzing   39
Anyone For Left Overs?   41
I'm Going On A Diet   42
There Once Was A Journalist   43

WORK
Application   46
I'm Handing In My Notice   48
The Office Bitch   50
Swedish And P.E.   52
A Broken Man   53

BEHAVIOUR

D.I.Y.ing It Again	56
I'm D.I.Y.ing It Again	57
Shoe Shop Heaven	58
The Wooo Hooo Girls	59
Exercise	60
The Dentist's Chair	61
Racial Attack	62
Thousand Mile Stare	63
A Tribute To Archie	64
Jumping The Queue	66
All Chewed Up	67
Depression	68
Mr Nic O'tine	70
I've Done It	72
I'm Trying To Write	73

CUDDLES, COBWEBS AND COCKERELS

Freddie	76
The Greedy Guide Dog	77
The Cobweb	78
That Fucking Cockerel	79

THE AGEING PROCESS

Night Time Visits	82
Growing Older Gracefully	83
Plastic Bits	84
Knocking On 60	86

Hull

The inspiration for my first two poems came in 2010 when I attended a poetry workshop run by the local performance poet Joe Hakim. Everyone was asked to write a poem about what Hull means to them.

The 'Clipper Race' referred to in verse 5 set off from Hull in 2009. The atmosphere in the city was electric.

IT'S GOOD INNIT?

This is Hull – wot we got?
Sanitisation, deprivation
Unemployment, no motivation
Teenage mums, no inspiration
It's good innit?

This is Hull – wot we got?
Beggars on street
Coppers on beat
No fishing fleet
It's good innit?

This is Hull – wot we got?
Queen Victoria on a toilet
Shops to let
Places to bet
It's good innit?

This is Hull – wot we got?
Cat on mat
Manky flat
Baseball hat
It's good innit?

This is Hull – wot we got?
Clipper Race
Saving grace
Smiling face
It's good innit?

This is Hull – wot we got?
Boats, planes
Theatres, trains
Museums, drains
It's good innit?

This is Hull – wot we got?
Intelligent people – generous, kind
Independent thinkers with an open mind
Is the rest of the country completely blind?
It is good in Hull – innit?

WHO DO THEY THINK THEY ARE?

Many Hull people are aggrieved
At the way they feel that Hull's perceived
If Southern Softies are to be believed
Hull should never have been conceived.
Just who do they think they are?

We don't have Kew Gardens or the O2 Arena
St Paul's Cathedral or the tennis for Serena
But, there's more to us than Chavs in trackies
Or Burger and Chips at Ronald Mackies.
Just who do they think we are?

We don't need posh shops to get our kicks
Like Harrods and Tiffanys or Harvey Nicks
We've got Primark, Poundland and pick 'n' mix
And a late night pharmacy for a methadone fix.
Just who do they think we are?

Hull's heritage is strong and its people are tough
We can laugh at ourselves when the going gets rough
And now we're saying we've about had enough
Of the snipes and the digs from the 'not-know-enoughs'
Just who do they think they are?

So what makes us different, what makes us renown?
How come we think we're Yorkshire's jewel in the crown?
Well, we coped with the Blitz without going down
And the floods and recession with barely a frown.
So who do we think we are?

Well, we think we're quite special and caring and strong
We think our history says we belong
To a group far from the back of beyond
So who do they think they are?
Who are you? Who are you? Who r ya who r ya?

The last line refers to Hull City fans who taunted the Manchester United fans with this chant after Hull scored against them during their brief spell in the Premier Division. (It back fired in the end when they were relegated only 2 years later)

Relationships

A NICE YOUNG MAN

I wrote this poem for a friend who is absolutely lovely but for love nor money cannot find 'a nice young man'

I think I've done the best I can
To find myself a nice young man
I've joined up to gyms and gone on courses
I've even considered joining the forces
The agencies charge a significant fee
But they cannot find the man for me

When I first signed up I was full of hope
But the first I met was clearly on dope
The second's personal hygiene was well below par
So *that* relationship didn't get far
The third was what you might call tight
I bought my own drinks for the whole of the night
The fourth was a bore – he had no conversation
Apart from his recent separation

But I kept on going – I didn't give up
Even though the fifth was ugly as fuck
And with the personality to match
Neither was the sixth a catch
And the seventh – well he drank a bit
But worse than that, he was a miserable git

The eighth looked good – had I found romance?
But with his Mum in tow there wasn't a chance
By the ninth I was starting to despair
Did I want a man with bright green hair?
At least he might be a bit of fun
But he was far too quick to grope my bum

So I'm wondering where to turn to next?
Do you need a bloke? asked a friend by text
Well, one advantage might be the sex...
But then again, if he's like my ex...
He'd leave me waiting at the station
As he steamed forth to his destination

I wondered 'Am I being too fussy am I being too shy
Are my expectations way too high?
For wanting a man who is socially able
And doesn't eat like a pig at the dining room table
Does such a man really exist?
Are there too many essentials on my find a man list?'

Anyway, I ventured on to my 10th attempt
Who was truly gorgeous though rather unkempt
He doesn't complain if I don't want to talk
He's really happy just to go for a walk
He's pleased to see me when I come home
He doesn't need me to text or telephone
He really is my ideal male
And I know he loves me when he wags his tail

UNREQUITED LOVE

I met this guy… it came out of the blue
Didn't expect it… well, you don't do you?
As soon as I saw him I started smiling
And… well… you know… fantasising

About his tight little bum and his nice broad chest
I'm sure there's no need to explain the rest
I found myself shaking with pure desire
This guy had set my heart on fire

I couldn't take my eyes off him
Wanted to rip his clothes off and feel his skin
Kiss his lips and snuzzle him
Run my fingers all over him

Wanted to stroke his cheeks and tangle his hair
Wear fantastic underwear
Wanted to seduce him and play him along
Put on music to discover 'our song'

Wanted to drag him to bed and make love to him
Basically climb all over him
My emotions wrapped in physical pain,
Wanting him over and over again

Since we met I've lost my reason
I'm like an animal come into season
Can't concentrate to do my job
At the drop of a hat I start of sob

I'm choked on unrequited love
The worst thing is I think I'm being a mug
We've exchanged numbers but he never phones
My friends are sick of hearing my moans

But it was obvious that he felt it too
His eyes were saying 'I want you'
So I had a few drinks and gave him a call
He barely needed persuading at all

He booked us a room in this posh hotel
One of them where you can ring a bell
Get room service… all of that
But I suddenly sensed this guy was a rat

Something told me that he was a sleaze
He'd done this before and he'd done it with ease
It was time to treat him to the female freeze
So I kept my knickers on and locked my knees

And, girls, I wish you could have seen the shock
When I confronted him about his… you know what
I said, 'has no one told you that size does matter?
I'd get more satisfaction from a sausage in batter'

Yes, I cut that prat right down to size
In the Endowment Stakes he'd won last prize
I made it clear he was out of luck
And retired to bed with a stonking good book

DO YOU?

Do you...

Give yourself a real hard time?
Your work and home life try to combine?
Never have the time to enjoy good wine?
Feel like life has lost its shine?

Cook lovely meals when you get home?
Have that housework cleaning syndrome?
Never feel like you've got it right?
Feel like life is fairly shite?

Dig the garden 'til your back is breaking?
Tell your partner that you've been faking?
Get sick and tired of all that baking?
Feel like a lunatic in the making?

Take the children to lots of activities?
Pay out for them to enjoy festivities?
Make their costumes for nativities?
Start to question your own abilities?

Ever say 'no' to other's demands?
Always bow down to their commands?
Wish you'd got another pair of hands?
Feel like no-one understands?

Can you....

Remember what life was like before you had kids?

THE HONEYMOON PERIOD

The honeymoon period soon wore thin
Just a matter of days after he moved in
He showed no interest in my long term ambitions
He immediately down-graded my living conditions

He quickly eroded my self esteem
He made it clear who was head of the team
For my hard work there was no respect
He completely ignored how well I dressed
So I threw my high heels in the bin
And had I dared… he'd have followed them in

Surprisingly my Mum didn't see
The detrimental affect he was having on me
He ingratiated himself into her affections
She was utterly blind to his imperfections
When I dared to complain about the physical demands
She said, 'for God's sake, Catherine, give him a chance'

My financial position was quite a strain
Without a shadow of doubt it was him to blame
When he went out he wore the latest styles
Then covered his greed with designer smiles
I had to forego what I desired
So he could have what he required

He had no inhibitions about making a fuss
In a shop or a restaurant or on a bus
His table manners were quite appalling
So why did others find him enthralling?
If it was anyone else I'd have shown him the door
But he'll maybe improve… by the time he's four

IS IT ME?

All my friends have been lying to me
Motherhood's isn't all it's cracked up to be
Wherever I go my baby goes too
He even accompanies me to the loo
Being a parent is over-rated
To my child I'm articulated...
Is it me?

There's no time for me to just be me
I can't settle to read or watch TV
Never before have I felt so important
Or impotent
Inadequate
In shock...
Is it me?

I should have taken more Precaution
Before signing up for Exhaustion
I yearn to get a good night's sleep
And take my time whilst I drink and eat
My life is chaotic,
Shambolic...
Is it me?

Of course I am responsible
For the life which I made possible
But it doesn't help that stupid Betty down the road
Has got 4 kids already and seems to cope...
It must be me

Surely I can't be the only one
Who wonders where their life has gone?
Yet my friends all seem to lap it up
Get excited when their kids use a cup
'He's crawling already – how about yours?'
Smugly superior utter bores...
It can't be me!

Ouch! That hurt – he bit my tit
That's the last time I'm feeding my little shit
He can have a bottle like all the others
And I won't be providing him with sisters or brothers
Hang on a sec – he's cut a tooth
I'm off to brag to that cow Ruth
I'm going to lie, I'm going to simper
'He's cut a tooth without a wimper
How about yours?'
This is Me!

I'm going to hold a coffee morning
And join the ranks of the inexorably boring
I'm going to spin them such a line
There's never been a child like mine
I'll tell them that he's started talking
For the first time he said 'Mummy' this morning
And look at him he'll soon be walking
He's decided to avoid the usual crawling
I toilet trained him within just one day
Is there any other way?
He's the most advanced child in the room
But I really should be going soon
I'm taking him to the toddler's gym
Then onto the mother and baby swim
Being a mother is enormous fun
Especially when you've got such a brilliant son
How about yours? ... Oh, what a shame!
No, of course you aren't the one to blame!
Must dash, bye for now
I never knew I could be such a cow!
This is the mother in me!

HE'S GOING TO GET IT

Just wait 'til he gets home tonight
He's going to get it – yeah, that's right
'Cos now I'm saying I've had more than enough
Of his behaviour making my life rough
Of him using all the hot water for showers
And waking me up at ungodly hours
Leaving wet towels on the floor
Well, I'm not taking it any more
He'd better change his ways... OR ELSE!

I'm his unpaid personal secretary
Because I do all that's necessary
To make his life as smooth as can be
But am I appreciated? No, not me
I do all his cleaning up
Wait upon him hand and foot
Write his letters and answer the phone
I'd find it easier to live alone
Just wait! Oh, yeah – he's so going to get it!

He considers me to be a soft touch
It wouldn't enter his head he's asking too much
I've been a door mat, a walk in the park
I'm the mug on which he's left his mark
But it's going to stop and it's going to stop now
And I'm really struggling to understand how
I've allowed this to continue for so very long
How come I managed to get it all so wrong?
But he is so going to get it. Oh, yeah... he is so going to get it!

For far too long I've been far too kind
I'm going to give him a piece of my mind
I won't be cooking him a meal tonight
I'm downing tools till we get this right
I'm sick of him taking me for granted
With his attitude I'm disenchanted
He only ever considers himself
People like him – they're only out for themselves
Oh, yeah he is so going to get it.

Well I can see him now he's coming up the path
Grinning his head off – I'll soon stop that
But he gets in before me like he always does
And now it's impossible to make a fuss
Like butter wouldn't melt he offloads his day
'Hiya, Mum, I got an A today
For writing a poem – about you
What's for tea?'...

He's done it again hasn't he? Got away with it... again.
How can I do anything now?
Just wait 'til tomorrow!

I'M LEAVING YOU

I read this next poem at The Hull Freedom Festival in 2010. Judging by the response of the audience it hit the spot with quite a number.

How many times do I have to say 'I've had enough, goodbye'?
If I stayed here one more minute I'd curl right up and die
I'm leaving you for freedom, I'm going back to live with Mum
Where I won't be judged or criticised and I won't be frowned upon

When we first met I was besotted – you really seemed to care
You advised me on my make up and how to style my hair
You threw out all my short skirts, high heels and low cut tops
And thoughtfully replaced them with shapeless dowdy frocks

That was just the start of it over time it grew much worse
You criticised my friends and you said they were a curse
You told me that my college course was a waste of time and effort
But when I left to please you, you were violent and aggressive

I really started to believe that I'd got my values wrong
When I think about it now I wonder how I stayed so long
You told me I was getting fat and you'd knock me into shape
Well you certainly did that all right you big fat useless ape

It didn't matter what I did you abused me more each day
You turned the heat and lighting off and checked upon my pay
You started drinking all day long then you started taking drugs
Your so-called mates who came around were just a load of thugs

You criticised my family – you said they took advantage
You even said you'd seen my father looking down my cleavage
When you accused my Dad of that you made me want to vomit
With that filthy lie and more besides you went beyond the limit

The sad truth is of course that we never stood a chance
Your family have different standards – it's obvious at a glance
So when you start to criticise you should look close to home
'Cos they're the ones responsible for the nasty seeds they've sown

You've controlled my life for far too long and you've done it all through fear
So get this message loud and strong 'I'm leaving you, my dear'
I need to be with people who've more intelligence than you
Instead of feeling sick each day about what next you're going to do

I don't want to live in a cold, cold house with not enough to eat
If I stayed here any longer you'd doubtless have me on the street
Don't try to tell me I won't survive I've heard it all before
I just wish someone had told me that you're rotten to the core

No, the one who's going to struggle here will certainly be you
I can manage without the insults and the verbal put downs too
For years you made it oh so clear that you thought I was inferior
Well now it's lesson time for you 'cos I'm definitely superior

Go find yourself another mug to take on all your baggage
I think you'll find that this girl here is smarter than your average
I doubt that you'll be strong enough to get yourself cleaned up
But from me at last I'm pleased to say – 'get lost and sling your hook'

Me Dad

This is written in the Derbyshire dialect. 'Snap' was the local word for a
packed lunch and became accepted as any lunch or snack. The word 'snap'
originated for packed lunches when the miners would take their 'snap' in a
tin work and the tin would 'snap' as it opened and shut.

Me Dad worra a miner 'un straight as a die
He wa' the role model I live me life by
'Ay up me duck,' wa' t'Derbyshire greeting
To one and all at t'corna place meeting

'E were an 'ard werkin man wi' the scars to prove it
'E wore a lamp on 'is 'ed so's 'e cud see da'an pit
Me Mum ud pack 'im up wi 'is bread and drippin' snap
Or lard and salt – wot d'ya think abaat that?

There wa' no money but I remember one time
He 'ad a white fiver which med 'is face shine
'Luk at that ar Cath – it's a five pound note
Don't tell nobody an' I'll bet it on t'tote'

Yeh, 'e liked a bet and a trip t' races
He liked t' see th'osses put through their paces
I went wi' 'im wi' me bag o' snap
We 'ad 'ard boiled eggs and me dad wore 'is cap

We went t'London – just 'im an' me
He tuk me wi' im t'see t'Derby
'Luk at that ar Cath, it's t'Royal Procession
Them's the nobs to the Royal Accession'

'E wa quite a bloke in 'is 'ard werking way
Every bill 'e 'ad 'e never failed t' pay
'E cud garden reight gud and 'is tomatus wa' grate
An' 'e gev me me snap wi' 'is tomatus on t'plate

When 'e'd finished 'is day da'an in t'pit
E'd gu t'pub t'wash da'an t'grit
'E'd 'av' a few fags t'gu wi' 'is drink
An' when 'e came 'om' me mum 'ud think…

24

'One more day done and one less to go
Da'an that bloody pit where no man should go'
'E werked da'an t'pit for 50 odd years
When I think of 'im na it fills me wi' tears

m. Mullen.

ODE TO THE FLAT CAP

That morning seems like a life time ago
I'd got up early and was raring to go
It wasn't far… I'd checked on the map
But my heart sank when I saw Bloody Flat Cap
Driving in front of me doing twenty eight
Completely oblivious he was making me late

Then came the caravans, lorries, red lights and tractors
A horse box and diversion were amongst the factors
I swear that between them the Gods had conspired
To delay my journey to ensure I got fired
So I honked on my horn and I flashed my lights
But Flat Cap ignored me as he admired the sights

I soon discovered Flat Cap had his own special style –
Every 10 minutes he travelled a mile
Behind him I grew hot with frustration
Please, please use acceleration
Then I suddenly considered the lifestyle I was leading
Was I in my right mind? Was I living? Was I breathing?

I'd spent years chasing around like a headless chicken
And not once in my life had it made my heart quicken
Then I looked across at Flat Cap and got this overwhelming feeling
The guy was FIT, wow… what a dish – he sent my senses reeling
Before he could say 'Flat Cap' I had conjured up a meeting
And very, very quickly I enamoured him through tweeting

Yes, my Flat Cap wearing fella I did cleverly pursue
His feet had barely touched the ground when he agreed to say 'I do'
We've organised the wedding and Flat Caps are the theme
We've planned to have it video'd – it's going to be a scream!
A string of pure white flat caps will be the ribbons on the car
And I'll wait till after ceremony to disclose my… Bipolar

The Bride and Groom and Bridesmaids and every wedding guest
Will all be wearing Flat Caps to ensure they look their best
The guard of honour will be composed of Flat Caps held aloft
And every single female there will have her fingers crossed
As she hopes to catch my wedding flowers and land a bloke like mine
Then we'll celebrate together, wearing Flat Caps, drinking wine

So when you meet a Flat Capped bloke don't presume that he's a geek
He might be what you're looking for – he could be positively sleek
He may be rich he may be poor but he never will be boring
For my own experience is there will be very little snoring
Lately we've been planning to have some little Flat Capped minors
Then we'll all be doing 28 in our Soft Topped Morris Minors

MY DAUGHTER IS GETTING MARRIED

My daughter is getting married – and what a carry on
The Invitations
The Venue
The Guests
…Her Dress

The Bridesmaids
The Best Man
The Ushers
….Her Dress

The Groom (mustn't forget him)
The Cake
The Caterers
…Her Dress

The Cars
The Presents
The Favours (never heard of them before)
…Her Dress

The Flowers
The Speeches
Our Outfits
…Her Dress

The Service
The Panic
The COST
…Her Dress

My outfit
My outfit
Her Dress
My outfit

Signing the Register
What Me? I'm flattered – That's Special - Thank You

In the end it was worth the carry on

SWEARY MARY

*This is a tribute to my sister Mary who was a successful novelist and a heavy smoker. I've called this poem 'Sweary Mary'... 'cos she did!
The end syllable of the last word in every line is to be pronounced like the 'ary' in 'Mary'*

Mary, Mary so contrary
Wrote her books without a dictionary
Painted scenes with vocabulary
Mary, Mary, literary

Mary, Mary so contrary
Researched facts for fictionary
Her writing was exemplarary
Mary, Mary imaginary

Mary, Mary so contrary
Behind closed doors was sometimes sweary
Her 'f's and 'b's they made you wary
Contrary, Scary, Sweary Mary

Mary, Mary so contrary
Baked great cakes with lots of dairy
Her Christmas feasts were legendary
Mary, Mary culinary

Mary, Mary so contrary
Smoked her fags without a carey
Coughed her way to the cemetery
Mary, Mary, nicotinary

Mary, Mary so contrary
You never were just ordinary
Barely collected your pensionary
Your demise was unnecessary
Mary, Mary, left too early

Nostalgia and Food

THOSE WERE THE DAYS

When I was little there was a corner shop
Where my mum would send me for the things she forgot
They'd even serve me with a packet of fags
'For my Dad,' I'd lie before I took a few drags
Those were the days

The local Co-op at the end of the street
Was a grocery store you'd be hard pressed to beat
They sold loose sugar in blue paper bags
And loaves of bread with 11 pence tags
That's 'd' not 'p'
Or 4 new pence to you and me
And they gave a dividend
To every member each year's end
The forerunner to the loyalty card
It helped us out when times were hard
Those were the days

In our town there was a baker
A cinema, an undertaker,
A 'wash and set' hairdresser
(She did her best – bless 'er)
A single shoe shop selling 'sensible' styles
High heels weren't appropriate for our lifestyles
A second hand shop – now an antique dealer
Back then dismissed as a wheeler dealer
Those were the days

Then we had a stroke of luck
A great big Woolworths opened up
Such a choice, such a treat
Where kids spent their pocket money every week
All sorts of sweets and chocolate bars
Soaps and perfumes in fancy jars
Toys and presents, stuff for the home
For the garden they'd sell you a grotesque gnome
Housewives bought their broken biscuits
To keep within their financial limits
Woolworths shopping epitomised
How the working classes were identified
Those were the days

The loss of those shops should be lamented
But no-one cares because Tesco's been invented
There's no broken biscuits on Tesco's shelves
Go take a look and see for yourselves
Now we're tempted by Tesco's Finest
Their impeccable cheeses and delicate wine list
Woolworths seemed like the poor relation
With their pick 'n'mix selection and in-town location
These are the days

It's sad we're losing our traditions
To the Multi-Nationals in powerful positions
Who had the foresight to visualise
What we're now starting to realise:
That they're taking over the world
I wish we still had the corner shop
Who'd remember your name and the things you forgot
Who'd take the time to ask 'how are you?'
The converse of today's 'bleeping' you through
Aah!... those were the days.

THERE WERE NO COMPUTERS

When I was a child we all walked to school
We were taught to swim in an outdoor pool
The girls wore skirts and the boys wore shorts
We learned mental arithmetic as matter or course
You see there were no computers

Dads went to work and mums stayed at home
Most of our clothes were hand knitted or sewn
None of us had heard of designer labels
But I can honestly say we knew our tables
You see there were no computers

We learned to cook and we learned to measure
We had music and art on Fridays for pleasure
We played sport for fun and we'd all compete
And it never occurred that someone might cheat
We didn't need computers

Everyone shared and the kids played out
If you didn't behave you were given a clout
We learned respect and to read and write
So somehow they got the basics right
Without the aid of computers

I think it's a shame that the kids of today
Have lost the art of how to play
That frightened parents won't let them play out
Because 'you never know who might be about'
So today kids need computers

We need mobile phones because we must 'keep in touch'
''Cos something might happen' but it doesn't – not much
We must have a sat nav in the car
Because we're bound to get lost if we go very far
We've a growing need for computers

So, I'd like to propose a computer free day
Just once a year – what d'ya say?
We could dig out the Monopoly and the Buckaroo
Play board games together like they used to do
Talk to each other face to face
Try living life at a reasonable pace

Drive the car and read a map
Well, that's pushing it a bit I'm not sure about that
Uuuummmmm... I should learn to use a computer

Well, 2 months on and I'm doing just fine
I've finally got myself on line
I gamble all day and shop all night
I've booked myself a cheap holiday flight
I've joined up to Facebook, YouTube and Twitter
I've put all my photographs up on Flickr
I've done all of this with a click of a mouse
Without even having to leave the house
I'm thrilled to bits with my computer

I've made friends with this soldier in Afghanistan
He sounds really nice and he loves his Gran
But she's not very well, not expected to last
And he'd like to see her but he's strapped for cash
And could I possibly help out?

I'm not very keen on computers
I'll bid farewell to computers
I got all excited but they're not for me
So I'm going to cancel my server fee

Would anyone like a computer?

MY MUM'S COOKING

Oh I just love a steamed sponge pudding
It reminds me of my mother's cooking
She served it hot with custard sauce
A cholesterol catastrophe as a second course

She made Bread and Butter Pudding and Bakewell Tart
Her Rhubarb Crumble was a work of art
She baked Apple pies and Lemon Meringues
Just thinking of them now gives me hunger pangs

For our Birthdays and special occasions
Her Sherry Trifles were the sensations
And if that weren't enough to fill our bellies
She'd sprinkle coconut on strawberry jellies

At Christmas time she was a master
At preparing meals without disaster
Into the Pudding she would mix
Lots of Silver Threpn'y bits

Yes, my Mum knew how to put on a spread
She always kept us kids well fed
And those thre'pny bits – I have mine still
A memorial to mum's cooking skill

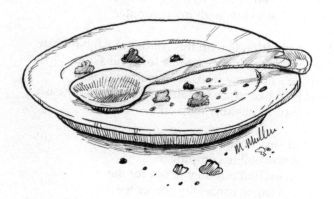

LET US EAT CAKE

I wrote this poem after watching a man in a local café enjoy his cake.

He held his fork
Savouring the thought
Anticipating the taste
Distancing the calories

His mouth watering
He delays
The first bite
Sips his coffee
Twiddles his fork

Trancelike
He moves his fork towards the cake
Breaks off a morsel
Slowly raises it
Opens his mouth

Controlled, delicious
Mmmmmmmmmmmm
MMMmmmmmmmmmmmmmm
Orgasmic
AAaggghh

Another mouthful
Bigger this time
And another
Mmmmmmmmmmmmm
MMMmmmmmmmmmmmmmm

Piece after piece
Faster and faster
'Til
Only one bite left
He hesitates
Waits
Anticipates
Salivates
Gobbles

'Let us eat cake'
MMMMMMmmmmmmmmmmmmmmmm
MMMMMMMMMMMMMMMMmmmmmmmmmmmmmmmm

DONCASTER BUTTERSCOTCH

Me Dad used to love goin' t'races
He loved t' see th'osses put through their paces
But Doncaster was special
They ran The St. Ledger
And Me Dad brought back Butterscotch just for me

Parkinson's Doncaster Butterscotch –uummmmmm!
An' if I remember right
The writin' were black and the boxes were white
Every piece were individually wrapped
In silver or gold little foily packs

It brings back memories of when I were little
Doncaster Butterscotch weren't chewy or brittle
It were smooth and creamy and it lasted f'ages
I savoured the taste as I ate it in stages
When I recall the taste of that very last sliver
It makes me taste buds go all aquiver uummmmmmmmmmmm!

Yes, the Parkinson family had got it sussed
But they just got on with it – they didn't get fussed
For me as a child it was the best taste ever
I wish Doncaster Butterscotch had lasted for ever

BUZZING

For many years we had both agreed
That when we retired we'd like to keep bees
We got all togged up and went to the training
We wore the suits without complaining

They showed us the hives after using a smoker
We saw the Queen but we didn't provoke 'er
They'd marked her up with the colour of the year
So upon inspection it was easy to see 'er

The Queen is bigger than the rest of the bees
She's got really long legs and exceptional knees
The job of the hive is to tend to her needs
To fetch and to carry as nature decrees

She lays eggs by the thousand day after day
Which the nursery bees tend in their own special way
They hatch into lava and are sealed in their cells
Then morph into bees as nature excels

We learned about swarming, workers and honey
To expect to get stung and not find it funny
They told us that mostly the drones are real lazy
But when Spring's round the corner they go kind of crazy

It's typical of males they're only after one thing
That's reproduction and sex on the wing
And the Queen isn't fussy she'll have any drone
Often more than a dozen before returning back home

She will brazenly display her erogenous zones
To those poor deluded sex starved drones
She'll regale them in sweet honey tones
And drive them crazy with her pheromones

When the deed is done the drones will die
They won't live to see their off spring fly
But there are no emotions to be shared
There is no sentiment in the insect world

Well we've bought a hive and all the kit
And we continue learning bit by bit
This hobby has truly bowled us over
If you'd like to view please do pop over

We're hoping this year to get our first jar of honey
It won't have come cheap – we're not in it for money
But with honey for breakfast and on muffins for tea
It doesn't take a genius to be able to see
Why we've fallen in love with the honey bee

ANYONE FOR LEFT OVERS?

The Christmas festivities have been and gone
But still the Left Overs linger on
When I open the fridge the only things I can see
Are the Christmas Left Overs staring back at me

There's left over turkey and left over pork
A bit of old sausage still stuck on a fork
There's a mountain of mash and some Christmas pud
Left over carrots, roast parsnip and spud
Left over sprouts and left over sauce
With the food in my fridge I could feed a horse

I've got left over beef and left over cheese
Left over trifle (too risky to freeze)
I've ate the mince pies, the chocolates and cake
I blame myself for the stomach ache
Anyone for Left Overs?

I've served turkey with salad and chips and spuds
I've made bubble and squeak and pies such
I've spiced it and curried it
Stir-fried and worried it
And now I just can't think what to do with it
Anyone for Left Overs?

The cat's disdainful she's turned her back
Saying 'fuck the turkey give me kit e kat'
The dog's turned his nose up the ungrateful sod
So it's down to me to scoff the lot
Unless... Could I possibly tempt you to join me with the Left Overs?

I am shamelessly inviting you over to mine
To ply you with food and seduce you with wine
We can make love by candle light 3 times before 9
I promise I won't mention your stomach line
Amidst the debris of the Left Overs

I'M GOING ON A DIET

I'm going on a diet, I'm determined to get fit
But first I must go shopping to purchase the right kit
I'll ask Ruth if she'll go with me – she's sound with her advice
Then we'll slip into café for a tea and custard slice

I need to get some trainers and some fancy little socks
Some shorts and track suit bottoms and one or two new tops
I'll pop into the book shop and buy myself some books
On diet and living healthily and how the gourmet cooks

I'm getting quite excited now we've fixed our shopping spree
Ruth was more than willing when she agreed to come with me
We're going to go to Meadow Hall and forget about the cost
And have a laugh together before the bankers call the shots

Well all that happened just last week now I'm living to regret it
Those fancy clothes and shopping means I've run right out of credit
I was full of good intentions when I decided to loose weight
But although my purse is lighter I will never be size eight

So now I have decided I must try a new approach
I'm going to my local gym to hire a fitness coach
I understand they've got a pool, Jacuzzi and a sauna
And outside there's a garden with lots of local fauna

And do you know they've got a bar with a well stocked cellar
And if I'm really lucky there'll be a lycra'd younger fella
Who will gently massage and encourage me as I attempt to get in shape
And together and with passion we will shift that extra weight

THERE ONCE WAS A JOURNALIST

I wrote this limerick after a meal out where a loud mouthed drunken journalist full of his own self importance really got on everyone's nerves – but being British – we said nothing!

There once was a journalist
Who went to a restaurant and got pissed
He was loud mouthed and rude
Conceited and crude
That pain in the arse journalist

Work

APPLICATION

Upon completion of this job application
Please forward direct to our administration
Along with 3 copies of your certification
As proof to the management of your qualification

When we've read the said application
We may possibly issue an invitation
With a time and date for interviewation
And in all probability – humiliation

We will question you on your education
Your hobbies, background and orientation
To add fuel to the fire of our investigation
We will also require a presentation
We will then decide if said presentation
Makes you worthy of our organisation

If appointed we demand dedication
Loyalty, long hours and appreciation
In return you'll receive remuneration
Which will not be open for negotiation

Thank you for attending your interviewation
At the appointed time in the correct location
We have considered the ideas in your presentation
And will use them to develop our organisation
We're unable to offer you employation
As the bosses son has returned from vacation
And because of the in-house collaboration
We have no need of your expertation

From: Mr Bare Faced Cheek and his Arse Hole Son

To: Mr Bare Faced Cheek and his Arse Hole Son

Thank you for your communication
Regarding the matter of my failed application
I'm pleased to advise you I've gained employation
At the local office of business taxation

Now it seems I'm under an obligation
To advise you of our investigation
For your business figures are pure fabrication
And you've fiddled your books for tax evasion

Can you guess where you'll be taking your next vacation?

From: Miss Smarter than you'll ever be – Rebecca Sian

I'M HANDING IN MY NOTICE

I'm handing in my notice
I'm on my way – I quit
I'm leaving, I'm resigning
I've had enough of it

The sad thing is you've just no idea
That you've created this atmosphere
Respect has gone there's only fear
It's time to change your ways, my dear

Working for you's been an education
Just a stone's throw away from humiliation
So today's going to be my graduation
For I'm sick and tired of your deviation

I've carried my load I've done my share
I've listened to you spouting hot air
I've done a good job and I've played fair
Well more than that – I've done it with flair.

I've had to learn lots of circus tricks
Like jumping around like a cat on hot bricks
How to get you out of a difficult fix
Keeping balls in the air – I've done it with six.

I can jump through hoops, I can hop and skip
I can turn cartwheels do a backwards flip
I've become an expert at tightrope walking
And balancing acts – well now you're talking.

I can stand on one leg spin a ball on my head
And oh, by the way – have the lions been fed?
I can act like a clown – for that I'm renown'
Or so I've been told after going round town.

I think that this poem says quite a bit
But there's one last thing before I quit
I've managed to rekindle my original grit
You insufferable self righteous little git.

THE OFFICE BITCH

Very recently Natasha won promotion
In the office she's caused quite a commotion
And I have to admit we said some nasty stuff
As to why she'd been appointed instead of us

'It's favouritism pure and simple
She's got long blond hair and a cheeky dimple
She wears her skirts short and gets in early
Those classic signs should have made us wary'

At breaks she takes him a coffee and bun
Leans over to reveal the shape of her bum
Wears low cut tops that are far too tight
I wonder where she sleeps at night?

That dental work must have cost of packet
And who do you think paid for that jacket?
And just look at her shoes – they're Jimmy Choo's
Oh my God! They're Jimmy Choo's!

Her computer skills are poor by comparison
To overweight, bespectacled Alison
Her telephone manner is not the best
But that's less important than her double 'D' chest

Her toe and finger nails she paints bright red
Her intention was clearly to lure him to bed
She resolutely ignored all the other girls' glares
As she fixed our boss with hypnotic stares

For 3 whole months did our boss resist
But Natasha had staying power and did persist
She savagely exploited her feminism
To achieve what's known as 'the management position'

But Natasha had reckoned without Fiona
The boss's wife with the bull dog persona
She soon sniffed out The Office Bitch
Chewed her up and spat out the bits

Natasha was no match for the likes of Fiona
The boss's wife with the Bull dog persona
Who dealt with Natasha as a matter of course
Then served her husband with a file for divorce
Before settling herself down to watch TV
With a satisfied smile and a large G & T

SWEDISH AND P.E.

Smiling and proud you wore your cap and gown
To the award ceremony in the heart of town
With your exam results you're overjoyed
And it won't be long till you're employed
You're very happy with your honours degree
In your chosen subjects of Swedish and P.E.

The hard work's done, you're on the up
And understandably you're ma's made up
Then she flattens the mood with her heavy sigh
'To repay your loan you must aim high
You'd best start applying, send off your CV
To the best known companies and the BBC'

6 months down the line and your hopes are fading
It won't be long till your skills need upgrading
It's all gone wrong for your career
And the reason my dear is blindingly clear
There is no call for Swedish and P.E.
If only you'd graduated vocationally

You could have been a plumber like your dad
Such a prospect now wouldn't seem half bad
But your parents didn't want that life for you
An education they said was the best way through
But necessity declares you must take a job
So you start stacking shelves for just a few bob

And actually you find that it's really O.K.
You're employed and useful at the end of the day
You're gaining experience you make friends with the staff
You go out together have a drink and a laugh
You meet up with Sophie the work place flirt
Who proves herself dextrous as she unbuttons your shirt
You were always confident your Swedish and P.E.
Would come in handy – eventually

A BROKEN MAN

I am
a bro   ken man
Getting by   the best I can
Kicked in the gut
Told to   shut up
Stand   up
Sit down
Lie   down
Bow   down

Redundant
Unim   portant
No longer   required
Got no life   Got no wife
Gone for good
Married f   or Worse
Not for   better
She sent me   a solicitor's letter
Marriage   vows
Broken   now

I'm   all over the place
Lost
                    The cost
                                        My life

No longer required

Behaviour

D.I.Y. ING IT AGAIN

My husband is D.I.Y.ing it again
Over the years he's driven me insane
When on the face of it a job seems simple
He can make it flourish like a teenage pimple

In every room his tools lie scattered
But it's the one that's missing that really matters
Every time it's the flaming same
He puts things down then can't find 'em again

He's a damned annoying bad tempered guy
It's clear I'm a suspect but I can't think why
The hunt is on and his face is like thunder
The doubts creep in and I start to wonder

When was the last time I used that saw?
Was it in the garden like the time before?
Have I left it parked next to the spade?
It probably is my fault it's been mislaid

'Cup of Tea?' I ask to relieve my guilt
What's that they say about milk being spilt?
A bit later on when it comes to the crunch
He decides he'll start the job after his lunch

Next he switches the telly on
And I know the day's lost 'cos it's O'Sullivan
'Is it worth it?' I ask myself
'All I wanted was a kitchen shelf'

I'M D.I.Y. ING IT AGAIN
(Husband's reply)

My wife's behaviour has changed recently
She's been flirting with me outrageously
I'm not complaining but I know the score
It's that D.I.Y. job she's mentioned before

Of me she has high expectations
But she doesn't understand the complications
That when doing one job it leads to another
And I can't do one without first doing t'other

She 'just wants a shelf' and that's O.K.
I intended doing it anyway
Eventually
Honestly

But I can't find my saw and I know it's her
Because I have searched for it everywhere
She'll never admit it she'll swear it was me
But she's definitely guilty 'cos she offers me tea

While I got the advantage I put the telly on
My luck is in it's O'Sullivan
He scores a fantastic 147
Watching O'Sullivan is snooker heaven

My wife observes me with her hands on her hips
And I turn it off without a word from her lips
From my adult I've become decoded
I feel like a child who is being scolded

So I collect my tools including the saw
And resignedly I get on with the chore
At this minute she's got the better of me
But she don't half make 'a nice cup of tea'

SHOE SHOP HEAVEN

I have spent my entire day in Shoe Shop Heaven
I couldn't decide which pair to buy so I just bought... 27
When I tell my husband I'll be sparing with the truth
I will simply say 'I've bought some shoes'

I have to admit I panicked a bit when I saw how much I'd spent
But on reflection a shop like that is quite an accomplishment
And now I've had the time to sit and think and get it all worked out
I'll present my news in such a way he'll never think to shout

The shoes will be delivered tomorrow when my husband is at work
I'll cook him a meal, ply him with wine, wear those strappy high
        heels and *flirt*
Then... when he's heavily inebriated and conclusively seduced
I'll produce for him a cat walk that will leave him... all confused

And on the off-chance that he is annoyed I've got a back-up plan
(And this one's never failed me yet in a battle with my man)
At first I'll smile, then apologise and explain I couldn't resist
Next I'll cry, say I'll return every pair – at which point he will insist
That I keep the lot, he's enjoyed the show and he couldn't care less
        'cos he's pissed

Over the years I've devised this winning formulation
Sex, food, wine and tears prove successful deviation
Then, when my husband's guard is down and he's starting to relax
I'll produce another cat walk – but this time... wearing hats!

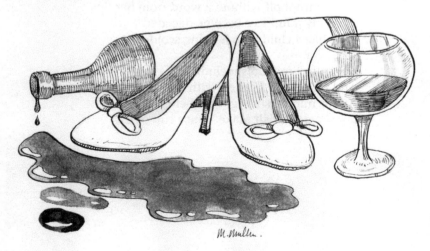

M. Mullen.

DINING OUT WITH THE WOOO HOOO GIRLS

Dining out – one of life's pleasures
Good food and company in equal measures
Shown to our seats by staff who're polite
Everything's set for a wonderful night

Then the wooo hooo girls arrive excited and loud
They sit themselves down at the next table to ours
They wooo hooo their entrance in celebration
Of their friendship, divorces and liberation

They're dressed up to kill, lip-sticked and young
For sure tomorrow they'll be over hung
They're pissed as newts and the night's just started
But alcohol's important to the broken hearted

Wooo hoooo! they scream with every move
I can't help wondering what they're trying to prove?
They get increasingly loud as the night wears on
My friends all agree – it's time we moved on

But just for a joke we decide to join in
Together our wooo hoos make a right old din
We get this wonderful rush of adrenalin
And before we know it – the whole restaurant's joined in

We look at each other – we're getting a buzz
Though we know this behaviour's not appropriate for us
But we're all over 60 and we don't give a stuff
And even the manager's woo hooing with us

Now much to our husbands' dismay
We've joined the wooo hooo girls of today
We're newly converted
They've all been alerted
We rehearse several times every day

Wooooo Hooooo!

EXERCISE

Bend and stretch and touch ya toes
Exercise until ya glows
Windmill arms and run on the spot
Exercise until ya drop

Run and jump and hop and skip
Exercise until ya drip
Hula hoop and twist and turn
Exercise until ya burn

Jump out of bed and run round the block
Get back home by 6.00 o'clock
Ride ya bike then have a swim
Exercise will keep ya trim

Press ups, lunges, stomach crunches
Boxercise and throwing punches
Martial arts (such discipline)
Exercise will get ya thin

Aerobics, dancin', keep on tryin'
Exercise will get ya cryin'
Burn another calorie
Exercise is agony

Rowin' throwin' climbin' jivin'
Is this what they call survivin'?
Pour that beer, pass them crisps
Exercise is for the dicks

THE DENTIST'S CHAIR

As I lie here in your dentist's chair
Into your face I pleadingly stare
Oh, please don't say I need a filling
Oh, please don't let my teeth need drilling

Then suddenly as I lie in your chair
I discover religion and utter a prayer
'Please find no problems as you search
And if you don't I'll go to church'

I promise I will floss everyday
I will brush to keep the decay at bay
Never again will I eat a dessert
If dentistry disaster it will avert

I feel like I'm frozen, I just can't move
As you prod around each and every groove
The relief is immense when you finally say
'No treatment required – that's it for today'

I float as I rise from your Dentist's chair
And into your face I thankfully stare
Oh, thank you for saying I don't need a filling
And for sparing me from your love of drilling

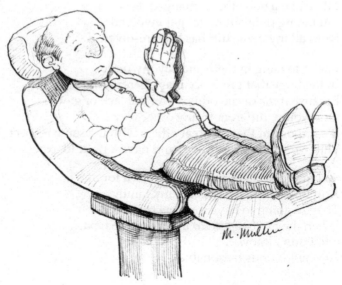

RACIAL ATTACK

I've been subject to a racial attack
Just because my friend is black
Such a lovely bloke, intelligent, kind
The perpetrators were out of their minds

Such devastation they've left in their wake
Flash backs for me every time I awake
At night in my dreams I sweat and I shake
I'm wondering how much more I can take?

I've lost my faith in the human race
Lost the confidence to leave my space
At court I'm scared they'll see my face
But it should be them who feel disgrace

I refuse to tolerate their mindless prejudice
And for their sins I'm demanding justice
For their senseless violence
I will not be silenced

Small minded and dangerous is what they are
On my brain they've left an indelible scar
I can no longer listen to other folk's strife
It's made me re-think my entire life

So just for a while until I recover
I'll be like a book that's changed its cover
I'm taking time out to not get involved
Until all my own stuff has been resolved

I need to hang in there and say my piece
In the hope that prejudice may decrease
Because it makes no odds if you're black or gay
Or if you're different in any other way
It's important that we treat others with the same respect
That we want for ourselves and have a right to expect

So I intend to tell them how it's been for me
And how badly it's affected my family
They're going to have the time to reflect
When they're banged up inside for the next...
Oh, I don't know...
20 years sounds reasonable

THOUSAND MILE STARE

Harry doesn't have a comfortable life
No house or garden – no trophy wife
People look away when they see him round town
With his collar turned up and his head turned down
His coat is in rags, he's got holes in his shoes
No belongings to mention, no state revenues
He rifles through bins and he smokes dog ends
And nobody really comprehends

Most people would class Harry as being insane
But they can't see inside The Old Timer's brain
They cross the road 'cos he stinks of meths
They're unaware he's profoundly deaf
The clean and healthy with superior taste
View Harry as a loser and with utter distaste
'Have you seen that old tramp – cor what a pong!
We'll raise a petition to move him along
We can't have him here in our neighbourhood
With our property values – well, it doesn't look good'

What a sad reflection on the Human Race
To judge by appearance and deny the space
To the likes of Harry who fought in the trenches
Who's deaf as a post and sleeps on park benches
Should you look in his face you can see he's not there
He's got that sad, far away, one thousand mile stare

That Thousand Mile Stare – the poor old sod
Who folks pass by without so much as a nod
They don't want to know, they don't want to see
But for the Grace of God – there goes me

TO ARCHIE

A tribute.

Such a lovely man
A kindly man
A 2nd World War Veteran

He made me weep at the words he spoke
And I quote:
'What happened to me
Has been with me
Every second
Of every minute
Of every hour
Of every day
For 50 years'

He was suffering from P.T.S.D.*
Battle related – military
The army insulted his integrity
When they falsely accused him of mutiny
Upon his character they imposed a slight
Because Archie had never refused to fight
What happened to Archie was a travesty
He was sticking to his orders from Montgomery

He was a good man
An honest man
A 2nd World War Veteran

If you're interested look it up
The Salerno Mutiny – the army fucked up
Others also paid the price
Suffering P.T.S.D. for the rest of their lives
For them the army did its worst
Now there's a first
Not

Archie didn't have a choice
Conscripted along with other boys
For the army he was one of many
Cannon fodder at 10 a penny
Archie survived but his life was shattered
Now finally his ashes lay scattered

He was a brave man
A courageous man
A very, very special man
A 2nd World War Veteran

* P.T.S.D. – *post traumatic stress disorder – symptoms include nightmares, flashbacks, mood swings, hyper vigilance and unsocial behaviour*

JUMPING THE QUEUE

That cheeky bugger just jumped the queue
Wide-mouthed we all let him walk straight through
As bold as brass he marched to the front
I could scarcely believe he'd pulled such a stunt

To look at him you'd think butter wouldn't melt
Booted and suited with his briefcase and belt
Head held high all toffed-up and groomed
Our superior… or so he assumed

He'd got a nerve that cocky sod
Treating folk like he's some sort of God
Trampling on others just to get ahead
It was easy to see he'd been poorly bred

Brought up believing he's one of life's best
He's not learned much in the parental nest
Material needs they have provided
But in his manners he's not been guided

They haven't taught him our culture of Queue
To say 'be my guest' or 'after you'
'You go first' or even 'thank you'
His way of being is to think 'screw you'

A few years down the line I wonder how he'll be?
Will he have a wife who thinks similarly?
Neither considerate of the other
What a shock they'll get if she becomes a mother!

I hope they get twins who scream all night long
I hope their nappies have an awful pong
That'd soon teach 'em to join the queue
'No dear, it's your turn, I'll wait for you'

I'll hold that thought in my imagination
It provides first aid for my frustration
Whilst I focus my mind on retaliation
And kicking his arse into orbitation

Yes, he'll be sorry that he crossed me
'Cos I've been practising ka..ra..te
I'll teach that bugger to wait in line
When my foot connects where the sun don't shine.

ALL CHEWED UP

I'm getting all chewed up about gum production
I'm sick and tired of its wanton destruction
The streets are spattered with chewing gum suction
And it doesn't perform any useful function
Ugh!

When it's stuck to my shoe it drives me insane
Yet no one is willing to take the blame
I can't get it off, I pick and I poke
This chewing gum problem is beyond a joke
Ugh!

And I've never understood what it's all about
I mean - chewing stuff up and then spitting it out?
The States should be ashamed of their exportation
It's nothing short of an abomination
Ugh!

I want to recycle the 60's campaign
'Keep Britain Tidy' went the refrain
I want to call out 'don't you dare'
To folk who stick their gum everywhere
Ugh!

I want a ban on gum production
I want to stop the wanton destruction
I want our pavements to be neat and clean
Not stuck up with gum unfit to be seen
Ugh!

To resolve this issue we should work together
If we don't do it now I don't think we'll ever
It's not that we can't it's more that we won't
But our kids won't thank us if we don't
Ugh!

So let us together fix up a meeting
And deviously plot the chewing gum beating
To knock on the head the bain of my life
And send it forever to the after life.
Yes!

M. Mullen.

DEPRESSION – DON'T TELL ME
ABOUT DEPRESSION

What's that you say – you feel depressed?
Don't tell me about depression
My depression could wipe the floor with your depression

Depression – did you say you've got depression?
Well, I know how you feel
Ooh! The things I could tell you about depression
Ain't it awful?

I look after my depression – it's important to me
Over the years I've nurtured it – been careful with it
I've even given it a name – Ron – it had to be male!

Yes, I know Ron like the back on my hand
I don't know what I'd do without him
How would I live? What would I do?
I've grown quite fond of my depression
It's safe – I know it – I'd be scared to lose it

I wonder - what would I have if I lost Ron?
Would I lose the other friends I depend upon?
Like my anxiety – that's Gerry
And my OCD – that's Phil
There's a definite pattern of male dependency!

Then the other day I met by chance
A woman who really understands
She told me that she'd been the same
Except her disorders had had a female name

We chatted on for quite a while
And I have to say I admired her style
'Cos although she was serious she seemed quite bubbly
She'd banished her disorders and was feeling... Jubbly

When I got home I had a row with Ron and Phil and Gerry
I told them all to pack their bags and move back home to Cherry
I watched them as they gathered their stuff and waved 'goodbye'
        as they left
And although on one hand I felt relieved – on the other I felt bereft

It's been hard going since we split but now I've found new friends
These fun guys that are moving in are bound to make amends
The first is Shane – better known as 'Shame'
Next is Dwayne – also known as 'Blame'
Last comes Angus in his kilt
Instantly recognisable and known as 'Guilt'
So you see I'm going to have an exciting life 'cos I'm clearly on the border
Of something better than depression – it's Complex Personality Disorder

MR. NIC O'TINE

I've looked at all the beautiful flowers
Enjoyed the wake despite the showers
Listened to the eulogy
He'd still be here if it wasn't for me

I smiled as he grew prematurely older
Smoking his fags and watching them smoulder
I embraced him as his blood ran colder
The calculating psychopath on his shoulder

For I am Mr Nic O' Tine
My attitude is kind o' mean
I used to whisper in his ear
'Go on – have one – you've nothing to fear'

Like The Bad Fairy waiting patiently
I tripped him up emotionally
'Just a quick drag – now isn't that nice?
And it's only one so it isn't a vice'

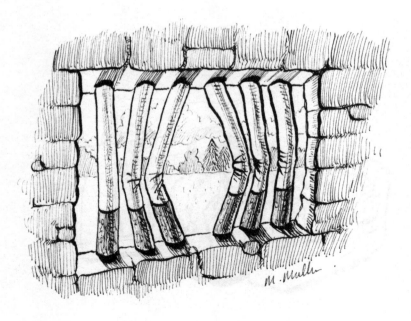

He knew without me his life would be harder
He'd never have coped with his increased ardour
And what would he spend his money on?
A new car? Holidays? Oh, come on!

He'd have just eaten chocolate and over-indulged
Had to join the gym to beat the bulge
And he didn't want to resort to that
When he could stick with me without getting fat

For years with his brain I conspired
To kill him off before he retired
He laboured under the misconception
That he'd live to receive his government pension
But I've been faultlessly mixed to achieve perfection
And prevented his recovery from that chest infection

All the big shots are on my side
Cyanide, formaldehyde,
Arsenic and carbon monoxide…
It's tantamount to suicide

If I were human they'd section me
And throw away the key...
Indefinitely

I'VE DONE IT!

I've done it! I've flippin done it!
I've quit smoking – I've done it!
For 4 whole weeks I've been smoke free
I'm going to celebrate with a spending spree

Going to get all those things I could never afford
Like nice clothes and shoes and a holiday abroad
I'm going to enjoy my shopping trip
And treating my son to that football strip

People tell me that I'm looking brighter
My eyes are shiny and my teeth are whiter
My sense of smell has returned full score
And I won't be stinking of smoke any more

My kids are really proud of me
When I struggled to cope they encouraged me,
'We love you Mum, just stick to the plan'
'Cos you can do it, we know you can'

I really believe I've achieved my goal
I feel like I've finally gained control
Of that awful addiction which shackled me
I can go where I like – I'm free, free, free

Because before I stopped I had to make a choice
Do I go out with my friends or stay in with my boys?
Nick and O'Teeny usually won
It was certainly easier but it wasn't much fun

What a drag to my friends I must have been
To refuse a night out 'cos of nicotine
How boring was I, what a sad sack
To stay at home with my 20 pack

Yes, I'm a reformed smoker – one of the worst
I think you should give up – dive in head first
I want you to know how good it feels
To be freed from the clutch of those nicotine wheels

I'M TRYING TO WRITE OR WRITER'S BLOCK

I need SILENCE
I need PEACE
Don't INTERRUPT
I'M TRYING TO WRITE

Don't ask 'how's it going?'
Don't stick your head around the door
I need it SHUT
With you on the other side
Forgive me, but
I'M TRYING TO WRITE

BACK OFF
Go out
Do anything but…
DON'T TALK TO ME
LEAVE ME ALONE
I'M TRYING TO WRITE

Don't be kind
Don't say a word
If you value your life never ever say
'I know how you feel'
'Cos you don't
I'M TRYING TO WRITE

So, I if you don't mind
If it's all the same to you
Just… BUGGER OFF

Cuddles, Cobwebs and Cockerels

FREDDIE

We knew our daughter had been feeling low
When she arrived back home with Freddie in tow
As he stared at us with big wide eyes
It was clear to see he was traumatised

We gave him lots of cuddles and hugs
Wrapped him up warm in snugly rugs
We bought him a bed and lots of toys
But he wouldn't play nicely with our other boys

As Freddie grew older he grew more demanding
He would completely ignore any reprimanding
He'd spread himself out upon our sofa
We had to say 'would you please move over'

Freddie became fussy about what he'd eat
He learned to distinguish the best cuts of meat
He refused to acknowledge my closest friend
He almost drove me round the bend

He started to prowl the streets at night
Picking up girls or starting a fight
Then the police caught Freddie on CCTV
I was really shocked when they showed it to me

There was Freddie in the local park
Having his end away each night after dark
I felt so ashamed I could barely speak
I took him to the vets the very next week

When Freddie came home he was so confused
He couldn't understand how we'd blown his fuse
From that day to this he hasn't strayed far
And I've kept his knackers – preserved in a jar

THE GREEDY GUIDE DOG

I wrote this poem after seeing a guide dog totally unable to resist a biscuit he found on the floor of a bus. He reminded me of the Labrador (Lizzie) we'd had years ago.

I'm a Labrador guide dog, strong and clever
I take my master out on his tether
We get about a bit – me and him
My diet and walking helps keep me trim

We go to the shops and to the park
I'm ever so patient, I rarely bark
But the other day when we got on the bus
I couldn't help but make a bit of a fuss

We'd boarded in the usual way
The driver said 'you don't have to pay'
Then from the corner of my eye I saw
A broken biscuit on the floor

Well, I was naughty I ignored the command
To sit and stay – 'cos that biscuit looked grand
I'm a Labrador you see I droo…oool over food
And with a chocolate biscuit I'm easily wooed

Within a few seconds the biscuit had gone
I searched but sadly there'd only been one
So I sat and behaved like a good guide dog should
And my master forgave me like a good master would

77

THE COBWEB

When I was created about a year ago
I was fine like silk I was all aglow
What the flies and the insects didn't know
Was that I was their enemy – a dangerous foe

For quite a while it felt O.K.
As my spider waited for flies to slay
But as he hung around he got more discontent
He got sick of waiting for a development

I couldn't move so I had no choice
I couldn't speak because I had no voice
I had to be patient just sit and wait
For the flies and insects to meet their fate

As time passed by and with no flies caught
My spider left me – he was hungry and fraught
I felt so lonely and full of self pity
Because my spider though grumpy had also been witty

And through the window I could see
My garden cousins in their finery
With their glistening dew drops on clear display
They would flirt with the sunlight and seductively sway

Over time I listened and observed
The householders as they ducked and swerved
My cobweb cousins in the sunshine outside
Were unaware of what happened inside

I listened in to phone conversations
Watched them as they struggled with relations
I knew the lies which they gave so boldly
And saw the reactions of those hurt so coldly

After a while I heard the bloke confess
'I should never have married, I'm in a mess
For the past few months I've had a lover
And the worst thing is dear – he's your brother'

So the peace of the house has been cruelly shattered
And outside my cousins look weathered and tattered
From all I've seen I could write a book
But I'll remain discreet in my cosy nook.

THAT FUCKING COCKEREL

When I first started writing poetry I made a decision never to use bad language. However further down the line, this was my first exception to my home-made rule. Sometimes only a swear word hits the spot. If you've ever been woken up at 4.00 a.m. by a cockerel in full cry you'll probably understand where I'm coming from.

I'm going to kill that fucking cockerel if he wakes me up again
Every summer morning he's up at 4.00 a.m.
He's done this to me too many times when I'm relaxed and sleeping
      sound
So I'm sure you understand that of his flesh I want my pound
That cockerel's gonna DIE!

This morning he had a lie-in – today it was 4.02
Then – cock-a-doodle fucking do, cock-a-doodle fucking do
I'm going to knock that cocky loud mouth right off his fucking perch
And I don't care if he leaves his chickens in the fucking lurch
That cockerel's gonna DIE!

I'm going to find out where he fucking lives and then I will I surprise
      him
'Cos he'll never hear a fucking thing as I manoeuvre in behind him
I'm gonna strangle that fucking bird just as he starts a cryin'
Cock-a-doodle fucking do, cock-a-doodle fucking dooooooooooooooooooo...

Well the murder was successful and today I got my sleep
'Cos from that fucking cockerel there was not a fucking peep
And when the farmer comes a calling I will keep my face dead pan
Because tonight for tea we're having cock-a-doodle coq au vin.

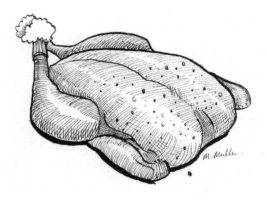

79

The Ageing Process

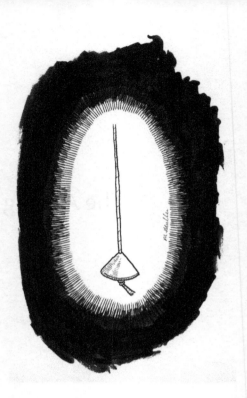

NIGHT TIME VISITS

I get up in the night to go to the loo
If it wasn't for that I'd sleep right through
Think how restful my life would be
If in the night I didn't need to pee

GROWING OLDER GRACEFULLY

As I grow older and I start to shrink
And my hearing and eye sight goes on the blink
Do you think there's any possibility?
That I might grow older gracefully?

Will my skin go all thin and papery?
Will I need a stick 'cos I walk shakily?
Will hairs start growing out of my ears?
But to be quite honest – that's the least of my fears.

I'm scared that I'll lose my reasoning
My memory, my home, my whole being
My dignity, confidence, ability
My status, character, personality

I'm worried I'll go into a nursing home
And I'll forget how to use my mobile phone
That I will become more argumentative
Hard to handle, difficult and aggressive

I couldn't stand to be fed pulped up food
Or be given drugs to placate my mood
I would have to change my attitude
From being obliging to downright rude

But I think growing older can't be all bad
People sort of accept it if you go a bit mad
They kind of expect you to lose your marbles
They'll say – 'she talks nonsense – she sort of garbles'

But I'm not there yet – no nowhere near
Yes, I've still got quite a few more years
And there's a guy down the road invited me to Bingo
And do you know… I think I'll go

Won't that upset the apple cart
Gran, on a date? – well the mucky old tart
Yes, I shall rock the boat deliberately
Because I intend to grow old ungracefully

I'm shall dye my hair bright blue and paint my nails bright red
And die drunk and dishevelled in my garden shed
At the reading of my will Bingo man will shout 'HOUSE'
Because he gave me a thrill when he felt in my blouse!

PLASTIC BITS
To be read as a rap

I was walking down the street just the other day
When I met this woman who had something to say
She said, 'Look at me girl don't I look fantastic
I got high heeled shoes and they're made outta plastic'

I got a plastic bag and a plastic purse
I got my husband this plastic nurse
I got my son this plastic tank
And I got it all paid for from my plastic bank

I got a plastic sofa and a plastic chair
I got plastic ta-ble-ware
I got plastic flower for my plastic hat
And I got my son a plastic cricket bat

I got plastic knees and plastic hips
I got a plastic nose and plastic lips
Yeah, I got lots of plastic bits
'Cos I love plastic to my finger tips

I got a plastic comb for my plastic hair
I got plastic boobs in my underwear
I got plastic nails and plastic teeth
When I die I wanna plastic wreath

When I'm gone I'll be a sensation
Cos I won't need formalderisation
I want my folks to remember my life
As the best plastic mum and the best plastic wife

KNOCKING ON 60

I've not made it a secret, everybody knows
That I'm knocking on 60 – that's how life goes
So now's the time to consider and reflect
Upon what I should do – upon what to do next?

Because although I'm 60 I've still lots to do
I want to travel and I want to pursue
My life with all its combinations
And I don't want to hear about my limitations

My husband's quite good – not the jealous type
I'd say his bark is worse than his bite
My family are all very special to me
Well… I did put them through my academy

I think it's important to mention my friends
Who are truly special and at times – godsends
When one of us struggles the others are there
And when one does we'll we say 'Good for her'

We all know someone who brags a bit
Says 'I don't look my age and I don't feel it
I only feel like I'm 22'
Well that's a thumping great lie – 'cos it's not possible

Yes, these days I admit it's not often I see
A bloke whose bum looks attractive to me
But when I do I get a sort of a lift
'I'M STILL ALIVE' – if you get my drift

So let all us 60's paint the town red
We don't want night nurse or breakfasts in bed
We want a life that's exciting and full
'Cos us 60's – well – we're incredible

Acknowledgements

I would like to acknowledge the support and encouragement I have received from Joe Hakim and Mike Watts who introduced me to writing poetry and to Cilla Wykes, editor of ThisisUll.com

Thank you to my family for 'being there' with special thanks you to my son-in-law Matt Mullen for his wonderful illustrations.

Thank you also to those brave individuals who have unknowingly contributed to my work.

Finally a sincere thank you to Clive Birnie of Burning Eye Books for being brave enough to publish this book

Write your own poems here: